Daisies, Dishes & the Desk

Dr Madhuri Goswami

Daisies, Dishes & the Desk © 2024 Dr
Madhuri Goswami

All rights reserved.

No part of this publication may be
reproduced, stored in a retrieval system, or
transmitted, in any form or by any means,
electronic, mechanical, photocopying,
recording or otherwise, without the prior
written permission of the presenters.

Dr Madhuri Goswami asserts the moral
right to be identified as the author of this
work.

Presentation by *BookLeaf Publishing*

Web: www.bookleafpub.com

E-mail: info@bookleafpub.com

ISBN: 9789363317222

First edition 2024

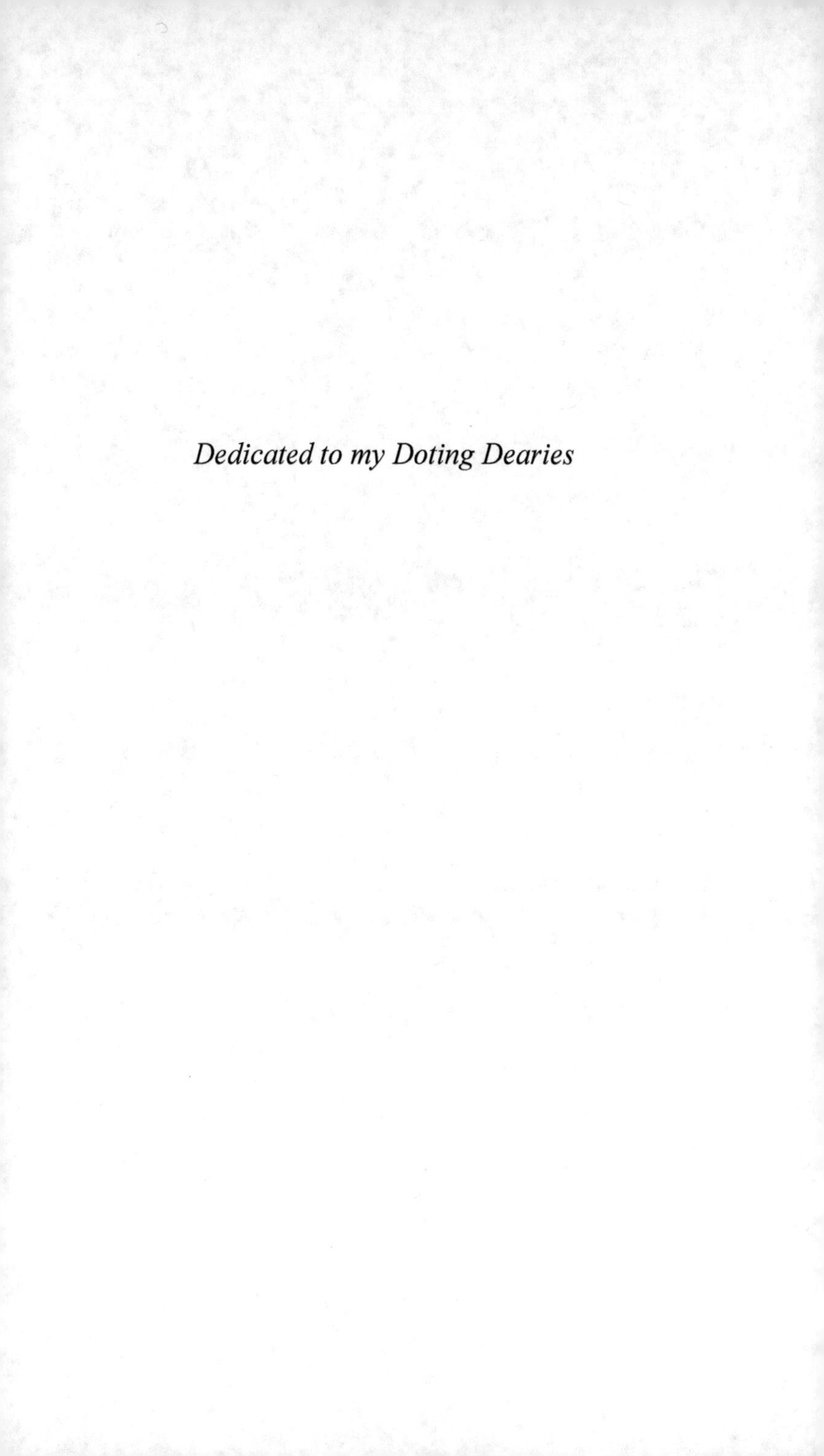

Dedicated to my Doting Dearies

ACKNOWLEDGEMENT

This collection of poems, "Daisies, Dishes & the Desk" would not have been in your hands without the encouragement and inspiration of many wonderful people.

First and foremost, I would like to express my deepest gratitude to the almighty for bestowing me with credo for creative writing. I am highly thankful to my family whose unwavering support and belief in my work have been a constant source of motivation. Their love and encouragement have been the backbone of my creative journey.

I am immensely grateful to my teachers and mentors, who have guided me with wisdom and insight, nurturing my passion for poetry and helping me refine my craft. Your feedback and guidance have been invaluable.

A special thanks to my fellow poets and members of my writing community, whose camaraderie and constructive critiques have pushed me to grow as a writer. Our shared love for the written word has been a great source of inspiration.

To the readers and supporters of my work, I express deep gratitude for your kind words, enthusiasm, and appreciation. Your engagement with my poetry gives it life and meaning beyond the page.

Lastly, I would like to acknowledge the beauty of everyday moments and the myriad emotions that have fueled my writing. This collection is a reflection of the world around us and within us, and I am grateful for the inspiration found in both the surreal and the tangible.

Dr Madhuri Goswami

PREFACE

In the quiet recesses of our minds and the vast expanse of our collective human experience, stories reside—stories that shape us, stories that move us, and stories that define us. It is with this profound understanding that I present to you this anthology of poems, a tapestry woven from the threads of countless narratives that have been whispered, sung, and written across the ages.

'Daisies, Dishes and the Desk' is more than a collection of verses; it is a journey through the heart of humanity, a journey that begins with the humble stroke of an author's pen and ends in the cherished embrace of a reader's heart. Each poem within these pages is a testament to the enduring power of storytelling, a reminder that in the ebb and flow of life, we find our deepest connections and our most profound truths.

From the brooding of a library book to the autobiography of a library clock, from the whispers of the morning breeze to the vesper's dusky grace, these poems invite you to explore the myriad facets of existence. They are a celebration of the human spirit, a tribute to the resilience of the soul, and a homage to the beauty of the natural world that surrounds us.

As you turn these pages, may you find solace in the tales of old, inspiration in the words of wisdom, and joy in the simple pleasures of life. May the verses within this book ignite your imagination, stir your emotions, and remind you of the boundless possibilities that lie within each of us.

So, dear reader, as you embark on this poetic journey, remember that every face tells a story, every heart holds a secret, and every poem is a key that unlocks the door to a world of wonder. Welcome to this anthology, where the human race finds elegance, timber, and harmony, and where every word is a step toward understanding the narratives of which we are all a part.

With warmth and anticipation,

Dr Madhuri Goswami

Daisies, Dishes and the Desk

Down by the daisy-strewn dell, I dwelt and
dreamed,
Drenched in the warmth of the dappled sunlight
gleamed.
Daisies flitted in the gentle breeze's sway,
As I whiled away the hours of the day.

The dishes lay forgotten, piled high and deep,
As I lost myself in a dreamy, daisy-scented
sleep.
But duty calls, and with a sigh, I rise,

To face the mountain of dishes, a daunting size.

Back at my desk, I tackle the day's tasks,
With determination, I don my metaphorical
mask.
But in the darkness of doubt, shadows creep,
As uncertainty whispers, threatening to seep.

Yet amidst the doubts, the darkness, and the
chores,
The daisies bloom, reminding me of life
outdoors.
For even in the depths of doubt's despair,
There's always a daisy, waiting to share.

So let us cuddle the daisies, the dishes, the desk,
And banish the darkness, doubt's daunting
burlesque.
For in the rhythm of existence, in its ebbs and
flows,
We find the beauty in every daisy that grows.

In the cadence of life's endless flow,

Amidst the chaos and the undertow,
We find the wisdom in each daisy's bloom,
A reminder that even in darkness, there's room.

For life's lessons are woven into the fabric of
time,
In the moments of cheers, in the moments
sublime.
From the daisy's resilience, we learn to stand
tall,
In the face of adversity, to rise above all.

The dishes teach patience, in their steady array,
As we tackle each challenge, day by day.
And at the desk, where dreams get a form,
We learn perseverance, in struggle 'n' storm.

But in the darkness of doubt, we find our
strength,
For it's in the shadows, we learn to go to any
length.
To believe in ourselves, trust in the celestial
energy,

And to forge on, with our dynamic synergy.

Let us clasp the lessons, the challenges, the
strife,
For it's in life's journey, we truly come alive.
And amidst the daisies, the dishes, and the desk,
We find beauty and worth in every lesson, every
task.

Just for Once...

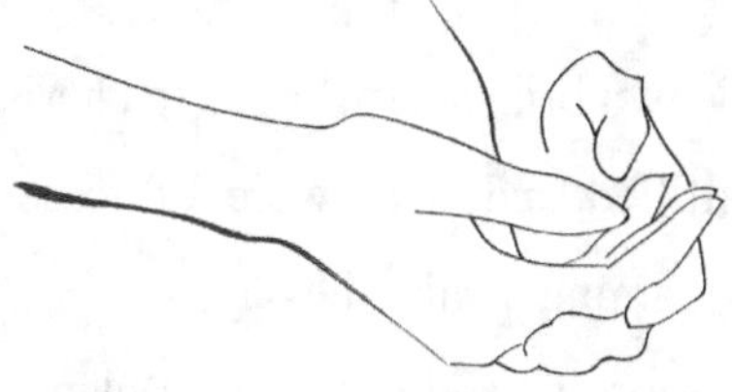

Peeking from floral facets, the life yearns,

For vernal times amidst bristly, prickly thorns.

Moaning eyes sometimes, other times cheerful

smiles,

Let's share the felicity with others, and go that

extra mile.

Just for once, at least once,

To turn a flower pot into a blooming expanse.

I have seen, and perhaps you have too,

The ocean grows fierce, breaking through.

Yet calm waves embrace the shore,

Let love be limitless, forevermore.

Widen its circle, let it soar high,

Touch tender hearts, reaching the sky.
Just for once...

Radiant dawn brings new hopes to cherish,
Some fulfilled, and many were left to perish.
Dusky gloaming awaits the day,
Crimson morning and ruby sunset play.
Murky night with moon's soft light,
How can one behold with eyes shut tight?
Spring of solitude, lullaby's sweet song,
Fetch energy, life force all day long.
Just for once…

Agreed! Darkness fetches awful fright,
Let's ignite lamps; make everything bright.
Candles for celebration, lamps for festivity,
Spread colours, bring back life's vivacity.
Colours of Holi, paths filled with cheer,
Steps in tune, togetherness near.
Each moment fresh, each moment new,
Paint the canvas of life in every hue.
Just for once...

Empty your heart, like paper plain,

Change your sight, and release the strain.

Let outlook shift, find scenes bright,

Feel inside out, harbour the blithe.

Just for once,

To turn a flower pot into a blooming landscape.

Silence speaks

In the deep

Recesses of the hearts,

Palate of thoughts

Grumbling, murmuring,

Echoes of mentation...

On one side, tacitly expressed,

But on the other,

Still suppressed!

Saying is an art!

Saying succinctly

Yet another prowess,

Sprucing jumbled pieces of thought-bits
Brings into a mosaic,
Involute amalgamation
Yet unnoticed.

I speak
Aloud
But,
Quiet inside.
I speak
When the walls are hushed
My silent soul finds
Its voice
When the air in the room heeds
Tune in….
The speech of silence.

In the deep recesses
Of the untold,
unexplored heart,
Murmuring echoes of mentation
Tacitly expressed, in silence
But...

Forcibly suppressed,

Amid uproar,

It's an unheard utterance.

My bosom holds secrets,

Veiled in quiet reflections,

A landscape of unspoken words,

Swirling

In a tempest of emotion.

In the stillness,

they find their form,

Gentle whispers,

tender thoughts,

Seeking a voice,

A way to be heard,

Amidst

The cacophony of the world,

Silence speaks.

A Road to Ecstasy

In the fields of gold, where sunlight weaves,
Where giggling laughter blooms among the
leaves,
Where pious hearts spread their wings to sheen,
Each fair moment gleams with a passion so
keen.

Happiness taps the door with gentle breezes,
It's a jingle, soothing murmur, hard to miss.
It's discovered in smiles, both grand and slight,
In shared bonds that both captivate and ignite.

It springs in the dawn's soft, first, rosy hue,
Also rays in the sky azure, a vibrant blue.
It whispers subtly in the quiet twilight,
A soothing tranquilliser, a guiding sprite.

Delight resides in giving selflessly, too,
In acts of benevolence, abundant or a few.
It blooms within instinctively, a sacred seed,

"

Nurtured by solacing words 'n' altruist deeds.

It's not a destination, but a way of living,
A journey filled with moments of winning.
In gratitude, its roots grow firm and deep,
In love, dream and hope, its promises keep.

So, let us avidly seek it, yonder or near,
In every simplest smile, in every tear.
For ecstasy, in its blissful, purest form sure,
Is found within, where hearts are pious and pure.

VESPER

Just as the azure grace yonder

Bids adieu to the crimson canopy,

That cerulean pious decency

Named as dusky maiden Vesper.

Darkening gradually and softly,

A witness of amalgamation

Of ablaze brightness and gloom,

fabricating its existence daily.

Though cognizant of the fact,

She hails Eos to perish, withered,

But neither gloomy nor illusioned.
Rather sways in her music wrapt.

Afore coalescing with the dawn,
Before leaving her ashen attire,
O' Maiden Eve! Be the matter,
Endow wings to the soaring Aborn!

Eventually emerges a thought,
From the solemn and splendid silence
Of her livid yet mellow/gracious face,
Holding the proximity of sought.

Born from the rudy golden aura,
Brings forth ascent out of the set,
The rising onset in the setting offset,
Awakening thoughts out of slept flora

Behold Eve's mesmerising mystery
Beacons and solaces the vital force
The domain of subconscious course
Weaves the texture of rapt reverie.

Followed by the pearls of words
To incarnate the mellow, mystic Muse,
Aye! The sapience arrayed in profuse
The thought turns into abstractions,

Measures spaces, gaps and distances
Fixes the long-awaited rendezvous,
Meditations excogitate the bridges
To fetch the far, aboard beloved kinfolks,

To envisage the doting affection
Suspending reality so far,
Now, wistful to return home afar
Feeling nostalgic and forlorn.

Just as the azure grace yonder
Bids adieu to the crimson canopy,
That cerulean pious decency
Named as dusky maiden 'Vesper.'

Aroma of Cinnamon

In the depths of my kitchen's spice rack,

I find a jar of cinnamon, fragrant and kind.

Its aroma fills the air, a warm seize,

As memories of recent events start to trace.

Just yesterday, as the morning broke,

I brewed a cup of coffee, a comforting stroke.

With a dash of cinnamon, I added a twist,

To awaken my senses, to give them a lift.

As I sipped the brew, its flavour profound,

I pondered the day ahead, what treasures I'd

found.

The cinnamon's spice was a reminder clear,

Of life's richness, of moments held dear.

In the deep thoughts of tasks to complete,

I paused for a moment, to savour the treat.

The taste of cinnamon, a sweet surprise,

In the midst of chaos, brought gentle ties.

And as the day unfolded, with its ups and

downs,

I carried the flavour, like a comforting crown.

For in every challenge, in every strife,

There's sweetness to savour, the spice of life.

So here's to cinnamon, in its warm ambience,

A reminder of repose, in any case.

For amidst the chaos, the stress, the strife,

There's always a flavour, in the spice of life.

She

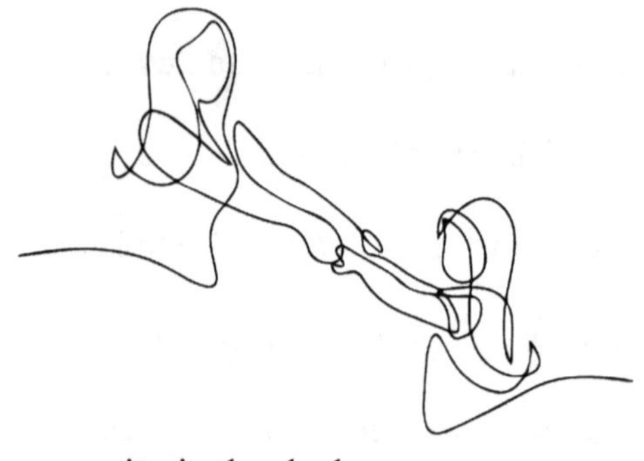

She, a warrior in the shadows,

Clutching her scalding soul close,

Lest her child lose ecstasy, faith and sleep,

She hides her grievances, unseen and deep.

Beneath layers of the illusion's circle,

She dreams of a distant oasis, a miracle,

Though breathing in the shadows cast,

She strives to make each moment last.

She swings on the pendulum's arc,

Life's journey, a relentless embark,

Built on sacrifice, on toil and strain,

Where blood, sweat, and tears remain.

She, the nurturer, the guardian, the guide,

Shielding her child from life's cruel tide,

Instilling hope with every smile,

In her love, she walks that extra mile.

She longs for a future, bright and bold,

Where her child's story will unfold,

Not in despair, nor in strife,

But as a blooming flower, full of life.

With crossed fingers and a steadfast heart,

She pens this verse, a humble piece of art,

A tribute to her strength, serenity and innate
grace,

In her world, fortitude and courage hold a loyal
place.

Is Life an Uphill Battle?

In the quiet chambers of your mind, you strive,
To chase your dreams, to keep them alive.
But amidst the whispers of doubt and fear,
Interference looms, drawing near.

Like a shadow cast upon your sunlit path,
It lurks in the corners, feeding on your wrath.
With every step forward, it pulls you back,
A weight upon your shoulders, a relentless
attack.

Yet still, you press on, through the darkness and
gloom,
Refusing to let interference seal your doom.
With determination burning bright in your soul,

You push through the barriers, toward your goal.

For in the struggle, in the battle fought,
You find the strength to rise, to conquer the
thought.
That interference, no matter how vast,
Cannot break your spirit, cannot outlast.

So you march on, with courage in your stride,
Knowing that within you, the power does reside.
To overcome the interference, to break free,
And reach the heights of possibility.

With every obstacle that stands in your way,
Gather strength to face it, come what may.
For though interference may try to impede,
You know within you lies the power to succeed.

So you press forward, with resolve unwavering,
Through storms of doubt, through trials never
wavering.
In the end, when the journey is complete,
You stand triumphant, victorious, upbeat.

Standing Alone

Oh, how it weighs upon my weary soul,

When no one sees the truth that I behold.

In every word I speak, in every breath,

I find myself alone, in silent death.

No matter how I try to make them see,

My thoughts are met with scorn and apathy.

Their eyes are blind, their minds closed tight,

To the convictions burning in my sight.

I stand alone amidst a sea of doubt,

My voice drowned out, my cries cast out.

No one understands the fire within,

The passion drives me, the battles I win.

But still, I persevere, though the road is long,

For in my heart, I know where I belong.

Though no one understands, I'll stand my

ground,

For my truth is mine, and in it, I'm found.

Oh! Hark! Dear Soul

O hark!

Gather yourself up!

When you are on the horns of a dilemma.

Just cheer yourself up!

Piercing the burnt sienna.

As you step into the worldly affairs

As you walk along the twisted lanes

Come across the bottomless pits

Toing and froing, at your wit's end.

O hark!

Never let your smile fade away

Just because of the appalling sight.

Never let you down, do stay

Sinewy, strong, staunch 'n' upright.

Never be the hapless prey of sway

Just because of the unruly foe.

Never let your heart shrink, pray

To feel the power of divine glow.

O hark!

In the whirlwind of uncertainty,

Stand firm amidst the storm.

Though doubts may cloud your clarity,

Let resilience become your norm.

Navigating through life's maze,

Finding paths both rough and smooth.

In the shadows of endless days,

Hold onto hope, don't lose your groove.

O hark!

Don't surrender to despair's call,

Even when darkness dims the way.

For within you lies strength to enthral,
Clasp the challenge, come what may.

Amidst the chaos, claim your intrinsic sway,
In every trial, in every unheralded scar,
Let courage be the torch-bearer of the way
Remember who you indeed are.

O hark!
With every step, with every breath,
Forge ahead with an unwavering state.
In the face of fear, stand tall, undeterred,
For you are the master of your fate.

Tiny Lovely Tots

When my heart goes out

in the midnight hour

Making an effort to scour

Some solace around

That window opens with a creek

A serene world peeps in

Shows a wide range of ideas

Dispersed by the stick of troubles

Scuffles, feud and fray.

The beauty that has been ignored,

Though not intentionally,

Yet unnoticed due to
bafflements or pressures.

Those tiny lovely tots
Remained ignored by fears,
Death, anticipation and
Mental haziness.

FLIPSIDE

In the darkest nights, where shadows prance,

There's a glimmer, a whisper of chance.

 Amidst the turmoil, the chaos, the fear,

There's a flipside, waiting to appear.

In adversity's grip, we find our strength,

A resilience born from trials' length.

Through pain and heartache, we learn to heal,

To find beauty in wounds, in scars concealed.

Loss becomes the seed of love's true worth,

Failure, an impetus, a catalyst for a new birth.

For every setback, there's a lesson to learn,

A silver lining waiting to be discerned.

Let's not dwell in the shadows' faces,

But kindle the psyche, find solace in paces.

For even in darkness, there's a flipside bright,

A beacon of hope, guiding us through the dead

of night.

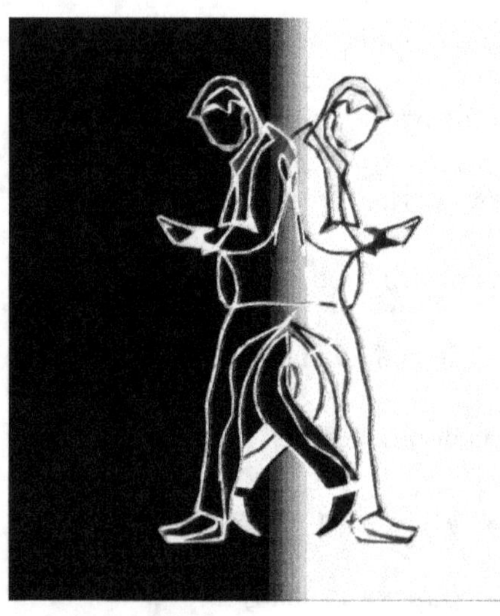

Altruism, a Selfless Creed

In selfless acts, a beauty lies,
Beneath the vast and open skies.
Altruism, a noble creed,
Where hearts reach out in times of need.

It's in the hands that offer aid,
In shelter from the storm's cascade.
A beacon bright amidst the dark,
A guiding star, a hopeful spark.

For altruism knows no bounds,
In every corner, it resounds.
It's in the stranger's helping hand,
In unity, we understand.

It's in the sacrifices made,
In giving without asking for aid.
A ripple in life's endless stream,
A selfless act, a heartfelt dream.

For in the giving, we receive,
A sense of purpose, to believe.
In lifting others, we ascend,
Our humanity, we defend.

So let us cherish altruism's elegance,
Be it in a bitty measure or be it dense.
For in its steering glint, we truly find,
The quintessential essence of humankind.

A Day Out with Flora and Fauna

In the soft halo of dawn,

With a sack full of hope

Mixed with anticipation

For the journey ahead.

The road stretched out before me,

Winding and narrow,

Leading away from the city's bustle,

Into the crux of the countryside.

As I travelled,

The landscape transformed,

From towering buildings to open fields,

Rolling hills adorned with patches of green,

And meadows dotted with wildflowers.

Each turn revealed a new vista,

An artwork rendered by Nature's hand.

In the depths of the forest,

Wandered and pondered,

Amongst ancient trees

That whispered secrets,

Their branches reached

Towards the sky,

A canopy of green

Stretching overhead.

The zephyr was lyrical

With the chirping of birds,

The rustle of leaves in the breeze.

In meadows bathed in sunshine,

I lingered, gazing and glancing

As butterflies gambolled on the breeze,

And bees hummed amongst the blooms.

Time seemed to stand still

In this serene landscape,

A world untouched

By the chaos of life, mundane.

As the day faded into evening,

I found myself by a tranquil river,

Waters reflecting

The resting tent of the setting sun.

In that moment of quiet reflection,

I felt the tranquillity

Wash over my soul,

As if I had found,

Reclaimed a bit of myself,

Lost in the simplicity and charm of that stroll.

Hail Music!

Hail Music, thou celestial, eternal gift divine,

Soothes every sheltered soul on its holy shrine,

Every tuneful note fills rejoices, claims a legacy,

With a symphony that lifts us to blissful ecstasy.

From yonder times, thou melodies have soared,

In every culture, thy lyrical magnificence is
adored,

Thou speak to hearts in a language pure and
true,

And in thy territory, we find our archaic spirits
anew.

The potent power of music, an energy so
majestic,

Weaves a spell across the land foreign or
domestic,
Whether in joy or sorrow, it finds its due place,
Bringing solace to every soul, as a life-saving
grace.

Life's tempests rage fiercely and doubts assail,
Thou revival touch helps to stand and prevail,
In harmonies, we find our strength and light,
Guiding us through the darkest of the night.

O Muse of music, with thy healing therapy art,
Thou heal the scars, wounds linger in the heart,
In every fresh chord, a spanking story is
unfurled,
A testament to the resilience of the human
world.

From the gentle lullabies, soothing a child to
sleep,
To the anthems, making the oppressed hearts
leap,

In every rhythm, a call for equality, unity and
peace,
A melody that bids all ceaseless conflicts to
cease.

The mighty power of music, a force to unite,
In its constituency, we find our common plight,
It speaks to all, regardless of creed or race,
A universal language, a harmonious embrace.

So let the music play, in every corner of the
earth,
A symphony of love, a celebration of our worth,
In its cadence, we find our shared tales and
songs,
A chorus of voices, to which everyone belongs.

O Music, thou art the voice of each existence,
In thy pleasing melodies, in thy sweet entrance,
In thy harmony, in thy terrain, culmination
awaits
So, let us celebrate thy eternal beauty and grace!

Lustres

In the quiet hours of the twilight's tranquil feel,

Lies a hidden charm, pure and gentle.

A lustre that emanates from within,

A soft glow that whispers of secrets akin.

It dances upon the surface of the sea,

A shimmering veil of tranquillity.

Each wave a ripple of silver and gold,

As the moon's tender glow begins to unfold.

In the depths of the forest, where shadows play,

There's a lustre that brightens the darkest day.

It flickers amongst the leaves, a gentle gleam,

A soft sheen that turns the woods into a dream.

And in the eyes of a lover, there's a lustre too,

A radiant glow that speaks of love true.

It shines with the warmth of a thousand suns,

A beacon of hope when the day is done.

So let us cherish the lustre that we find,

In the beauty of nature, in the hearts intertwined.

For in its soft glow, we find our way,

A guiding beacon to brighten each day.

Melody of Linguistic Euphony

In words, we weave, a language rich and deep,

A tapestry of sounds, a symphony to keep,

Yet in the twirl of vowels and consonants,

Lies the intricacies of linguistic hunts.

From Shakespearean verse to the modern
tongue,

The pronunciation game is hardly ever won,

For every rule, a myriad of exceptions,

Tripping tongues, causing subtle tensions.

In accents varied, from coast to coast,

The same word spoken, but somehow engrossed,

In a concord unique, a rhythm all its own,

A social struggle of speech, widely known.

But in this diversity, there lies a beauty,

A frolic celebration of humanity's unity,

In the tapestry of pronunciation's art,
We find the essence of each soul's part.

So let us encompass the quirks and bends,
In the way we speak, in the words we send,
For in the struggle of pronunciation's might,
We find the melody of language's delight.

In every syllable, a note does play,
A musical motif that transcends us away,
Through the highs and lows of linguistic flow,
In accents gentle, or with a fervent glow.

From the drawl of the South to the clipped tones
of the East,
Each variation, a harmonious feast,
In every intonation, a story told,
Of cultures rich, of traditions bold.

So, let the tune line of language ring,
In every word, in every song we sing,
For in its cadence, we find our song,
A chorus of voices, where we all belong.

Let's celebrate the beauty of linguistic grace,

Imbibed in every accent, mirrored at every face,

For in the symphony of language's euphony,

The human race finds elegance, timber and

harmony.

Under the Pipal Tree

In front of my home, where three narrow roads converge,

Diagonally Stands the Pipal, a sentinel of our cultural upsurge.

Its roots delve, as our family values do, deep into the earth,

An axis of spiritual rituals, a bystander of our festive mirth.

Its independent boughs reach towards the

boundless sky,

Embracing and cuddling the heavens, upright, as

if to defy

The circumference of mortal life, the constraints

of the earth,

As a testimony to resilience, a symbol of

constant growth.

Around its sturdy rugged trunk, a raised

platform was built,

A cemented circle, *Gatta*, a shelter, sacred and

cherished.

We play *Gatta*, a game of both skill and

afternoon leisure,

On the *Gatta* round the Pipal, a world for

innocent chatter.

With stones and pebbles, tossed and caught in
mid-air

On that sturdy platform, our laughter echoed
everywhere.

With quick hands, sharp eyes, each stone players
seek,

Traditions' joy, that time can't erase, though it's
meek.

But the tree stands more than merely a
playground's delight,

As a symbol of faith, devotion to Nature, and a
sacred rite.

Women gather in the morning light, with pots in
their hands

A devout, humble sight, to water the Pipal tree
sands,

Beneath its sprawling canopy, thirsty passers-by

find repose,

In the cool water of earthen pots, find a

quenching compose,

Stocked by my Grandma to fill the countless

cupped hands,

To succour, to beat the heat amid this dry, arid,

desert lands.

As whispers of the wind, through Pipal leaves, a

plea to pause,

To pep up, in the shade of Pipal, 'n' admiring its

noble cause.

Mesmerising with his symphony of ages, a

melody of time,

Echoes of the past glory, dispersing a motto of

life sublime.

In the shade of the Pipal, weary seekers find

peace,

As its presence brings solace, a sense of release.

It stands as a witness to the passage of years,

A sturdy yet silent observer, dispelling all fears.

Oh, Pipal tree, your perennial presence is a

promise to keep.

A testimony to endurance, fortitude, and values

rooted deep.

In your retreat, exists a timeless, peaceful,

embrace,

A sanctuary of wisdom, a sacred subsistence.

Around the Clock

In the family library, I stand tall and proud,

A silent sentinel amidst books stacked high and

proud.

With hands that tick and tock, I measure time's

flow,

In this haven of knowledge where stories come

and go.

From my perch on the mantel, I observe it all,

The laughter and the tears, the rise and fall.

Each day unfolds in the pages of this room,

A sanctuary of stories, where memories bloom.

In the morning, as the sun gently streams,

I awaken from slumber, to fulfil my timeless

trances.

With each passing hour, I mark the moments

dear,

As readers come and go, drawing near.

Families gather 'round, sharing tales of old,

As children listen wide-eyed, their imaginations

bold.

I watch as pages turn and minds flee in

ingenuity,

Lost in worlds of wonder, quest and eternity.

But amidst the warm fuzzies, there's a tinge of

sorrow,

For time is fleeting, with no promise of

tomorrow.

I witness the passing of days and years,

As the seasons change, and life appears.

Through the highs and lows, I remain steadfast,

A constant companion, as the years slip past.

Though my hands may age, and my gears may

wear,

I'll keep on ticking, with steadfast care.

For in this family library, I have found my place,

A keeper of time, in this sacred space.

And as long as there are stories to be told,

I'll stand tall and proud, as time's stronghold.

Every Face Has a Story

Every face has a story carved within its lines and
contours,

A tapestry of life, where each experience serves.

The trace of laughter, in the wrinkle of an eye,
remains

A monument of happiness, amid life's refrains.

A furrowed brow speaks of trials endured,

Moments of struggle, of fears reassured.

The gentle slope of a smile, a silent shrug,

Reflecting love's warmth in a tender hug.

Marks and scars, each telling a story
of moments they fell, of battles fought bravely,
As in the rise from every fall, there's a glow,
An account of courage, in the heart's steady
flow.

Eyes are windows into the soul; they contain
secrets deep,
Treasured memories, vivid views and vows to
keep.
Scars and marks, each with a tale to tell,
Of battles fought bravely, of times they fell.
But in the rise from every fall, there's a glow,
A story of courage, in the heart's steady flow.

Eyes, windows to the soul, hold secrets deep,
Memories cherished, and promises to keep.
In a fleeting glance, a history unfolds,
Of dreams pursued, of destinies foretold.

Each face a canvas, painted by time's hand,
A unique masterpiece, in life's vast land.

So as we meet eyes in the daily parade,

Remember, every face tells a story conveyed.

Look beyond the surface, see with the heart,

Understand the narratives, of which we're a part.

For in every visage, there's wisdom to glean,

A reminder that every face has a story unseen.

What a Book Thinks!

In the hallowed halls of the public library, I
reside,
A modest and profound book, with stories to
confide.
Bound in leather, my pages weathered and worn,
I've witnessed the ebb and flow since I was born.

My tale begins in the hands of the author's pen,
Crafted with care, from beginning to end.
From the printing press to the library's shelf,
I've journeyed far, imparting wisdom and
wealth.

As readers come and go, I silently observe,
Each one unique, with stories to preserve.
There's the young child, wide-eyed with wonder,
Exploring worlds unknown, as they plunder.

Their fingers trace my words, with eager delight,
Lost in adventures, from morning 'til night.
Their laughter fills the air, a jubilant sound,
As they immerse themselves in tales profound.

Then there's the student, with books piled high,
Searching for knowledge, reaching for the sky.
With furrowed brows and pens in hand,
They delve into my depths, to understand.

Their annotations fill my margins, a testament
true,
To their dedication, and their thirst for what's
new.
They challenge my ideas, they question my plot,
But in the end, they find what they have sought.

Next comes the lover, with romance in their
heart,
Seeking solace in words, as they depart.
They lose themselves in passion's rejoice,
As they devour my pages, with intensive poise.

Their sighs fill the air, as they turn each page,
Lost in the beauty of love's sweet stage.
Their hearts beat as one, with the characters'
plight,
As they journey together, through day and night.

And let's not forget the elder, with wisdom to
share,
Seeking solace in stories, as they sit in their
chairs.
With eyes that twinkle and hands that shake,
They revisit old friends, with every intake.

Their memories intertwine with mine, as they
reminisce,
About days gone by, in a moment of bliss.

They find comfort in my words, as they turn
each page,
A companion in solitude, through every stage.

So here I stand, in the public library's enfold,
A witness to life's delights and trials, face to
face.
For in the hearts of readers, I find my home,
A testament to the power of words, as they
roam.

Hey, Idioms!

In a world of words, where meanings twist and turn,

English idioms thrive, each one to learn.

"Break the ice" and start anew,

"Hit the nail on the head" with truths so true.

"Let the cat out of the bag" and secrets spill,

"Burn the midnight oil" for dreams to fulfil.

"Spill the beans" with stories untold,

"Actions speak louder than words," be bold.

"Once in a blue moon," rare things appear,

"Every cloud has a silver lining" to clear.

"A piece of cake," when tasks are light,

"A blessing in disguise" turns wrongs to right.

"Raining cats and dogs," the heavens pour,

"Back to square one," we start once more.

"Beat around the bush" and never be clear,

"Through thick and thin," we hold dear.

"Let sleeping dogs lie," avoid the strife,

"Put all your eggs in one basket," risk your life.

"Cost an arm and a leg," so dear the price,

"Hit the books," for knowledge precise.

"In the nick of time," just at the brink,

"Jump on the bandwagon," before you sink.

"Kill two birds with one stone," be wise,

"Under the weather," when health's demise.

"Fit as a fiddle," in perfect shape,

"Bite the bullet," for courage to drape.

"Kick the bucket," when life's at an end,

English idioms, our language they mend.

They colour our speech, these phrases we keep,

"Out of the blue," they leap from the deep.

So, use them well, in the conversation's flow,

For, with idioms, our expressions grow.

Cerebral Fun with Pun

In a world of wit and clever jest,

Intellectual jokes are the best.

They make you think, they make you grin,

A perfect blend of brain and spin.

Why did the mathematician refuse to argue?

Because he couldn't find the right sine to pursue.

He knew that logic, straight and clear,

Would solve the problem, never fear.

A physicist walked into a bar,

And said, "I'll have a drink, but not too far."

The bartender laughed, and replied with glee,

"I serve drinks with uncertainty."

A philosopher and a chicken crossed the road,
Debating deeply as they strode.
"Why did you cross?" the chicken asked,
"To question existence," the philosopher basked.
A chemist sat with a periodic table,
Singing elements' names like a fable.
"Do you have any gold?" asked a knight in jest,
"Au, get away!" the chemist expressed.

A linguist and a poet had a pun,
Debating which language was more fun.
"C'est la vie," the poet softly sighed,
"Life's a pun in every tongue," the linguist
replied.

An astronomer gazed into the night,
With stars and planets shining bright.
"Why was the moon sad?" a child queried.
"Because it's just going through a phase," she
cheered.

A programmer with code so sleek,
Wrote a joke in Python, what a geek!
"Why do Java developers wear glasses?" he
jested,
"Because they can't C#," he confessed.

A biologist, keen on plants and trees,
Said, "Photosynthesis, if you please!"
"Why do plants hate maths?" she was asked in
the grove,
"Because it gives them square roots to solve!"

Intellectual jokes with a dash of flair,
They tickle the mind with knowledge to spare.
So share a pun, a quip, a wisecrack,
And watch the laughter echo back.

Unboxing an Attic Box

In the attic, amidst the dust and shadows,

Lies a box, weathered and forgotten,

Its contents are a mystery, locked away,

Holding secrets of generations past.

Within its wooden confines, whispers linger on,

Echoes of laughter, tears, and whispered
conversations,

A testament to lives lived and loves lost,

And the passage of time, relentless and

unyielding.

Perhaps within its depths, letters are tucked,

Yellowed with age, bearing secrets untold,

Words penned in haste or with careful intention,

Revealing the hearts of those who came before.

Or maybe photographs lie dormant,

Capturing moments frozen in time,

Faces smiling, eyes twinkling,

But what stories do they hold behind their

smiles?

And what of trinkets and treasures,

Gathered over years and miles,

Each one a fragment of a larger story,

Waiting to be uncovered and to be weaved

In its aboriginal place of genesis.

In that untouched box in the attic,

Lies the essence of a family's history,

A tapestry woven with threads of bliss and

sorrow,

A treasure trove of secrets waiting to be

discovered.

As the lid is lifted, the past unfolds,

Stories untangle, and every artefact entails a

saga

From yesteryears, revoking the legacy to be

cherished.

Cultures in the Sea Tide of Distant Lives

In the diaspora, a culture survives or thrives,

In the rhythm of the sea tide of distant lives.

Amid the foreign soil's grounding,

Their hold is firm and long.

Many may see this seemingly

Arbitrary act of defiance,

As merely a catchy tune, a song;

It is so much more than that—

It is the story of survival.

It bears a purpose,

Struggling, to be seen, to be found.

On the bright side, not stagnant,

Constant recuperation

In the flame of adaptation every single day.

In the cadence of language,

A story unfolds,

A tapestry of traditions,

A legacy to hold.

People tell stories in the language they use,

To preserve it

And sustain its traditions

Woven into the fabric of the universe.

From the old country's shores

To new horizons afar,

Its melodies and rhythms traverse every star.

The dishes teach patience,

In their steady array,

As flavours and spices blend,

Memories of home hold sway.

There, behind graceful arches

And in the tangle of a diaspora,

A symphony is heard.

They feel it is a celebration of their heritage,

the ground, harmonious for them.

So, let the cultural ramifications prevail loud and

clear.

This is what we yearn for

In every word of the tradition.

For therein lies our tune,

In the rhythm of the violent.

A parade of opinions is effective when everyone

has a say.

It is in that embrace of the diaspora,

A culture endures, revives and keeps on.

Cultivating a rich heritage,

Kinship it maintains.

Climbing the ladder of the unpredictable gust of

change

And the moments in time.

It is left to stand as,

Unyielding light in the alien land.

My Abode

Where whispers of the morning breeze carry
reveries from distant lands,

And sunlight paints with gentle strokes the
endless possibilities it commands.

Here, walls are woven of wonder, and floors of
soft imagination,

Where every step is a new beginning, a promise
of creation.

In this abode, time bends and weaves, to suit the
soul's desire,

Each moment rich with potential, each heartbeat
a spark of fire.

The garden blooms with rays of hope, unfurling
petals of possibility,

Where every thought becomes a flower, and
every dream, reality.

Here, the mind's eye sees beyond the realm of
the known,

Where horizons stretch infinitely, and seeds of
inspiration are sown.

So I live with Faith, in the house—not so grand
yet just and fair,

Where every corner invites the soul to wander,
wonder, and dare.

www.ingramcontent.com/pod-product-compliance
Lightning Source LLC
LaVergne TN
LVHW011050200726
843509LV00011B/1376